The Joy of Sisters

by Karen Brown

Handwritten inscription:

To Pat
With Love

This book has just some of the things I want to say...

Love always —
Judy

READON
PUBLICATIONS
INCORPORATED

W9-BJO-985

Library of Congress Cataloging-in-Publication Data

Brown, Karen
    The joy of sisters / by Karen Brown.
    p   ;   cm.
    ISBN 0-88166-295-X
    1. Sisters—Quotations, maxims, etc. I. Title.
PN6084.S56B76   1997
818'.5402—dc21   97-16066
                                                        CIP

Editor: Bruce Lansky
Editorial Coordinators: Michael Platzer and Steven Roe
Production Manager: Joe Gagne
Production Assistant: Danielle White
Photo Editor: Maggie Merkow
Cover Designer: Danielle White
Cover Photography (clockwise from left): © 1995 by Bill Lai. Used by permission of Photo Bank, Inc.; © 1997 by SuperStock; © 1997 by P. Beck/Frozen Images; © 1997 by SuperStock; © by Jim Whitmer; © by Jim Whitmer

This edition published in Canada.
Licenced by Readon Publications in agreement with Meadowbrook Press
100 The East Mall, Unit #15, Toronto, Ontario M8Z 5X2
Tel: 416-503-3444 Fax: 416-503-9386 Toll Free: 1-800-401-9774
Email: readon@readon.com Website: www.readon.com

BOOK TRADE DISTRIBUTION by Simon & Schuster, a division of Simon and Schuster, Inc., 1230 Avenue of the Americas, New York, NY 10020

01 00 99 98 97   10 9 8 7 6 5 4 3 2 1

Printed in Canada

Acknowledgments

We would like to thank the individuals who served on a reading panel for this project: Teresa Bateman, Margaret Park Bridges, Dorothy Brummel, Gail H. Clark, Faye Click, Tamera L. Collins, Olga Cossi, Holly Davis, Rebecca Dotlich, Nancy Flood, Ruthie Hawkinson, Laura Irvin, Sydnie Kleinhenz, Wendy Lees, Jean H. Marvin, Janet McCann, Ingrid McCleary, Barbara Merchant, Jeanne M. Nelson, Elaine Nick, Josephine "Joi" Nobisso, Elizabeth Paterra, Renee Paulson, C. S. Pederson, Reggie Platzer, Lori Reed, Joan Marie Saxon, Mildred Schantz, Rosemary J. Schmidt, Mary Scott, Irene Sedeora, Esther Towns, Evelyn A. Wade, Maryan Winsor, and Vicki Wiita.

We would also like to thank the photographers who contributed to this book: pp. 3, 10, 40, and 86 © 1997 by SuperStock; p. 15 © by Randy M. Ury/The Stock Market Photo Agency; p. 20 © 1997 by P. Beck/Frozen Images; pp. 25 and 65 © 1989 and 1995 (respectively) by Bill Lai. Used by permission of Photo Bank, Inc.; pp. 28, 33, 56, 74, and 81 © by Jim Whitmer; p. 47 © 1996 by Harry Cutting; and p. 93 © 1993 by RB Studio. Used by permission of The Stock Market Photo Agency.

Dedication

To my sisters,
Kris Marsh and Kay Fulton,
with love.

Introduction

Those of us with sisters know how lucky we are to experience this special lifetime relationship. From the secrets of childhood through the pangs of adolescence and on to the challenges of adult life, we know that we can count on a sister to share everything, to laugh and cry with us, to lend an ear or a helping hand, and most of all, to be a cherished and loyal friend.

The Joy of Sisters is a tribute to sisters everywhere, and I hope that in these pages you find something that will serve as a remembrance of your most treasured sentiments of sisterhood.

Karen Brown

Sisterhood is like electricity. It's an
invisible but powerful connection.

With sisters, the only strings attached
are from the heart.

The invisible ties between sisters
are often the strongest bonds.

Sisters together are a force
to be reckoned with.

You and your sister.
It's a win/win situation.

Selfless
Inspirational
Supportive
Trusting
Encouraging
Reliable
SISTERS

Your sister is God's gift to you.

When you have two sisters
you're twice-blessed.

Sisterhood is a celebration of life,
love, and family.

You don't get something for nothing,
except your sister's loyalty.

Your sister gives from the heart
and expects nothing in return.

Sisterhood is made up of small sacrifices—
and large rewards.

Sisters know that their relationship is based on give-and-take, and that sometimes one sister has to give more than her share.

Sisters know that the effort required in a relationship is like peeling an onion—it's a lot of work, and it can make you cry.

Nothing is so wondrous as the birth
of your much-longed-for child—
or the birth of your sister's.

No one finds your children as charming
and brilliant as you do—except your sister!

Sisters earn their place in heaven when
they take care of each other's kids.

For sisters, seeing their children carry on
family traditions gives hope for the future.

As sisters watch their children at play,
they realize that the more things change,
the more they stay the same.

Sisterhood is a sibling revelry.

Who says you can't go home again?
Wherever you and your sister are,
there it is!

Your sister knows that the most important
furnishing in a home is love.

Sisters are often the glue that holds
families together.

She walks on the wild side;
you, on the straight-and-narrow.
But when it comes to family,
you always meet in the middle.

Charity does begin at home. You can ask
your sister for favors that you'd never ask
of anyone else!

Blood is thicker than water, and you can
count on your sister when you need
a transfusion of confidence.

Older sisters offer footsteps to follow when the path seems confusing.

Younger sisters are grateful to older ones for paving the way for such important milestones as dating, curfews, and makeup.

As you travel the road of life, your sister can give you directions.

A smart sister knows that example
is much more powerful than advice.

Imitation is the sincerest form of flattery,
especially when a younger sister
emulates an older one.

Your sister believes you are wise,
especially when you come to her
for advice!

A wise sister tells you to always put off until
tomorrow what you shouldn't do at all!

A sister will tell you that it's important to
know how the wind blows, especially when
you forget to wear a slip.

Your sister can help you see that some
mistakes are lessons, not tragedies.

Your sister reminds you that a mistake
is proof that you tried.

A wise sister helps you grow better,
and not bitter, when faced
with disappointments.

A wise sister will encourage you to
keep trying in trying times.

When you're worried about what you *can't*
do, your sister points out what you *can* do.

When you feel like a wannabe, your sister
assures you that you already *are.*

Two's company,
especially between sisters.

Busy sisters *always* make time
for each other.

No matter how busy you are,
your sister always comes first.

Between sisters, familiarity breeds
contentment.

&

Sisterhood is the comfort of a "we"
instead of the loneliness of an "I."

&

An evening with your sister and a bag of
popcorn produces food for thought—
and for the soul.

One of the best home remedies for loneliness is a visit from your sister.

Your sister is always happy to see you—even if you've stopped by unannounced, and her house is a mess.

Smart sisters know when to visit, and when to keep their distance.

With a sister, no matter how old you are
you can still lapse into childish behavior.

Sometimes you and your sister are
children disguised as grownups—
giggling and whispering to see what
you can get away with.

When you're with your sister, you don't
have to act your age.

Sisters are never too old to giggle
like children.

❦

Sisters' laughter can turn into tears at jokes
no one else would understand.

❦

Smart sisters know that a good day is not
complete without laughter.

Sisters can have a rollicking good time
together doing absolutely nothing.

Sisters know that early to bed and early to
rise means that they'll miss all the fun.

Sisters know that to be totally sane,
they have to have moments of craziness.

Sisters know that anything worth having
is worth a shopping trip!

Your sister's closet has always been your
favorite place to shop—and, of course,
the price is right!

Your sister knows when it's your turn to be
on stage—and it's her turn to lead
the applause.

When you're on a winning streak,
your sister will be the first to greet you
at the finish line with a blue ribbon.

Your sister always wants the best
for you—and helps you do
whatever it takes to get it.

Your sister's words of encouragement are
often the boost you need to accomplish
your goal.

Your sister takes pleasure in your accomplishments as if they were her own.

Your sister brings out the best in you— and you in her.

Behind every great sister is another who cheered her on.

Helping your sister row to a far-off shore
gets you there too.

Your sister points out the beautiful scenery
as you travel the road to success.

Your sister will help you reach for the stars
to find a little piece of heaven.

Sisters know the importance of following
their hearts—and doing what they love.

Smart sisters know that life's greatest risks
also yield its best rewards.

You know that your sister will always go
the extra mile with you, even on an
unpaved road.

⚘

Your sister is there when you need
someone to lean on.

⚘

A wise sister knows when to lead,
when to follow, and most importantly,
when to walk by your side.

A sister's love can help lighten your load.

When your ship comes in,
your sister helps you unload it.

When there's work to be done,
your sister rolls up her sleeves.

When *you've* got a big problem, your sister
says, "What are *we* going to do?".

Your sister knows that two heads are better
than one—even if hers is barely above
water, and yours isn't screwed on right.

You can count on your sister to walk in
when everyone else has walked out.

When you're beginning to have doubts
about yourself, you can count on
your sister to believe in you.

When you're paralyzed by fear, your sister
gives you the self-confidence to take action.

Sisterhood is a lifelong conversation.

Conversations between sisters are like
a book that you can pick up at any time
and continue with ease.

With sisters' conversations, the well
never runs dry.

The most important rule of sisterhood is
to listen to each other.

The best thing about deep conversations
with your sister is that she really listens.

A sister's greatest gift to you
is her willingness to listen,
no matter how late the hour.

When your sister says, "Can we talk?" w
she really means is, "You talk. I'll listen.

A wise sister always tries to see things
from your point of view.

Your sister understands the words
that you don't say.

There are things you just don't have to
explain to your sister.

Blessed is the sister who knows when to
speak—and when to remain silent.

Sisters understand the silent language
of a warm embrace.

Between sisters, a silent touch
speaks volumes.

Your sister can make a statement without
saying a word by just raising her eyebrows.

As children, you hid your diary from your sister. Now, you *want* to tell her everything!

As children, you dreamed of a room of your own. Now, you can't wait to share a room with your sister—and stay up all night, talking.

You used to tell *on* your sister.
Now you *tell* her everything.

The most precious gift sisters can give to each other is themselves.

Sisters know that good news is better when you share it with each other.

With your sister, you can think out loud.

With a sister as your confidante,
you can be confident.

Like your hairdresser and your shrink,
you can count on a sister to keep your
deepest, darkest secrets.

Sisters know that a long talk on the
front-porch swing will always take
precedent over piles of laundry.

Quality time: you and your sister
confiding in each other
while washing dishes.

When you're between a rock and a hard
place, call your sister!

Your sister will discuss your latest dilemma
with you—at 2:00 in the morning!

Your sister is someone who will indulge you
when you need to rehash a gripe
for the third time.

Talk, talk, talk.
Talk is cheap, except when your sister
moves to another coast.

When it comes to fitting conversations into
a long day, sisters have developed talking
on the phone—while fixing dinner and
changing the baby—into an art form.

Your sister shares your tears
and your triumphs.

Sisters' shared life is like a seesaw.
When you're down, she's up for you.
And you take turns.

Sisters are grateful for having each other
to share life's storms and to enjoy
the calm that follows.

Your sister knows when you need to laugh,
to keep from crying.

Sisters know that sometimes the best
solutions to big problems are reached with
the help of cookies, chips, and ice cream.

When you're a sister, you sympathize,
console, and commiserate—that's your job!

Sisters know that a helping hand
is just a hug away.

Your sister knows when you need flattery,
encouragement, and a big hug.

When a sister is guilty of loving too much,
it's a crime of the heart.

When you want to run away from home, your sister's house is a good place to go.

You can take off your hat on a bad
hair day when you're with your sister.

When you've had a bad perm, your sister
brings you her scarf collection.

Sisters sympathize when you have a good
hair day—and nowhere to go!

Your sister convinces you that there's a beautiful swan in the mirror, when all you can see is a silly goose.

A sister's like a makeover artist— she brings out the beauty in you.

Your sister has 20/20 vision, except where your faults are concerned.

When you're on a diet, your sister
orders salad too.

Your sister offers to wash and let you dry
when she knows you've just had
a $25.00 manicure.

When you're busily feathering your nest,
your sister donates her ostrich boa.

Sisters are like your favorite slippers—
warm, comfortable, and cozy.

When you've got cold feet, your sister's
support feels like warm slippers.

When fishing for compliments, you can
count on your sister to throw you a line.

Having your sister just a phone call away is like having your own private therapist.

Meeting your sisters after work for a drink used to be called happy hour. Now it's more like group therapy.

Your thoughtful sister sends you
Valentine's Day roses when you don't
have a boyfriend.

Your sister gives you her umbrella during
a storm, then helps you see the rainbow
afterward.

Sisters know that when you sow
seeds of thoughtfulness, goodwill
begins to grow.

Sisterhood is like a choir: you may sing different parts, but still produce beautiful harmony.

Sisters may march to different drummers, but they can still dance to the same beat.

Your sister respects you for being yourself.

Supportive sisters appreciate their
differences as much as their similarities.

Sisters know the importance of being true
to themselves—and to each other.

Your sister knows everything about you—
and loves you anyway.

Wise sisters know what to notice in each
other, and what to overlook.

A considerate sister doesn't insist
that you see everything through her eyes,
but allows you to use your own.

You and your sister may have had a
difference or two—but never
an indifference!

Grown-up sisters have learned to disagree
without being disagreeable.

A wise sister honors your opinion—
even when she doesn't agree.

A gracious sister will meet you halfway—
even if she thinks you're half-baked.

Your sister is brilliant and sensitive when
she sees your point, and just a little
misguided when she doesn't.

Your sister can't really prevent you from
doing anything wrong. But she can keep
you from enjoying it.

A sister's forgiveness is a welcome gift.

A savvy sis knows that the one who apologizes always gets the last word.

Your sister will be quick to forgive your faults—especially if you reciprocate.

When you get too puffed up, your sister
will poke you and let some air out.

A wise sister helps you see that if you're all
wrapped up in yourself, it's not a pretty
package!

When you're caught up in a flight of fancy,
your sister's words can bring you
back down to earth.

When you need to read between the lines,
your sister hands you reading glasses.

It sometimes takes a savvy sister to help
you separate fact from fiction.

When you're making mountains out of
molehills, your sister will knock them
down to size.

When charmed by a face across a
crowded room, your sister reminds
you that you can't see without
your glasses.

Your sister will remind you of your rights
and your wrongs.

A supportive sister helps you find
the virtues in yourself, rather than
the vices in others.

Your sister gives you the kind of advice
you *need* to hear—not just what
you *want* to hear.

A sensitive sister offers criticisms in private
and compliments in public.

Your sister may be aware of your faults
but would never admit them to
anyone else.

You can count on your sister to talk about
you behind your back—and say
good things.

Sometimes the light at the end of the
tunnel is your sister with a flashlight.

A sister's love is like a candle that lights up
the dark places in your life.

When you're about to burn a bridge,
your practical sister makes you
cross it first.

When you're tripping down a dangerous
path, your sister pulls you up
to the high road.

You need a sister to help you out of the
difficult trouble that was so easy for you to
get into all alone!

When your life is in need of repairs,
your sister arrives with her tool kit.

Your sister helps you pick up the pieces
and mend a situation you thought
beyond repair.

Your sister never gets in your way, unless you're on the way down.

When you're finally at the end of your rope, your sister helps you tie a knot so you can keep hanging on.

Your sister's concern helps soften the blows when you've learned a lesson from the school of hard knocks.

Sisterhood includes sharing a burden that
becomes too heavy for one.

Between sisters, love may not
conquer all—but it can certainly ease
the pain.

Between sisters, stories of your childhood
never get boring—they just get better
and better!

Being with your sister enables you
to travel backward in time.

Home movies, dusty scrapbooks, and a
closet full of memories—sisters can turn
back the hands of time!

Reminiscing with your sister is like refinishing a fine antique: you carefully strip away layers of memories and chip away at family myths to get to the core of things.

Sisters know the fun of taking the skeletons out of the closet—and making them dance a little.

Between sisters, a rediscovered memory can cause goose bumps.

Sisters reminiscing: so many subjects,
so little time.

Loving sisters understand the joy
of a shared memory.

For sisters, the past is full of
Kodak moments.

Sisters always stick together through thick and thin—and dieting in-between.

Sisters know that you can grow old gracefully—or wear a very large muumuu.

A little white lie is okay when your sister asks if her legs are beginning to look like Great Aunt Bertha's.

Sisters often look at each other as if
in a mirror—with shared experiences
etched on their faces.

Sisters know that wrinkles are just life's
"Certificate of Achievement" for laughter—
and tears.

Your sister's remembrances are cherished,
but so is her ability to forget.

Sisters enjoy laughing together over
experiences that were once painful.

Sisters who grow old together realize that
all happiness has been obtained with some
degree of pain.

You and your sister used to know all the answers. Now you realize that sometimes you don't even know the questions.

Your sister said that one day you'd appreciate her—and now you finally do!

Sisterhood is a club with a lifetime membership.

Everyone should be their own best friend—
but it never hurts to have a sister
as a backup!

Diamonds are nice, but a *sister* is a girl's
best friend.

Your sister is there for you—
today and always.

Sisters know that, no matter what,
they will always have each other.

A sister will do anything for you—
any time, any place, any way.

Out of sight, out of mind? Not with sisters!

No matter how far away you live,
you and your sisters are always close.

Friends drift apart, pets come and go,
and neighbors move away, but the bonds
of sisterhood endure forever.

Order Form

Qty.	Title	Author	Unit Cost (CDN $)	Total
	Golf: It's Just a Game!	Lansky, B.	$14.00	
	Joy of Sisters	Brown, K.	$14.00	
			Subtotal	
		Shipping and Handling (see below)		
			G.S.T.	
			Total	

YES! Please send me the books indicated above. Add $3.75 shipping and handling for the first book and 50¢ for each additional book. Add $2.50 to total for books shipped to U.S. Overseas postage will be billed. Allow up to four weeks for delivery. Send check or money order payable to Readon Publications Inc. No cash or COD's, please. Prices subject to change without notice. **Quantity discounts available upon request.**

Send book(s) to:

Name_____ Address_____

City_____ Province/State_____ Postal/Zip Code_____

Telephone (_____)_____P.O. number (if necessary)_____

Payment via: ❏ Check or money order payable to Readon Publications Inc. Amount enclosed $_____

❏ Visa ❏ MasterCard

Account #_____ Signature_____ Exp. Date_____

Mail to: Readon Publications Inc.
100 The East Mall, Unit #15, Toronto, Ontario M8Z 5X2
readon@readon.com

Phone (416) 503-3444   Toll-Free 1-800-401-9774   Fax (416) 503-9386